Curious George®

The Donut Delivery

Dozen donuts please

Adaptation by Monica Perez
Based on the TV series teleplay written by Joe Fallon

George is always a good monkey—when he's asleep. But no monkey wants to sleep through Saturday. This was a Saturday that cried out for something special . . .

"Donuts!" the man with the yellow hat announced.

That was special. Next to bananas, donuts were George's favorite food.

"How about eggs with those donuts?" the man asked George. "Please count how many we have and write it down."

But when George looked for the eggs, he found there were none left to count. "There are no eggs?" the man asked. "Why didn't you write zero?" George didn't know how.

The man with the yellow hat sat George down with some paper and a pad.
"See, George," the man said, "zero ALONE means no eggs. None.
But zero after other numbers makes them mean a lot more.

If we put a zero after one, that's ten. Write another zero, and that's a hundred."

George stared hungrily at the zeros. They reminded him of donuts!

Luckily for George and his empty stomach, they headed out to buy the groceries. The man stopped in front of a market. He said, "I'll go in here and buy eggs while you get the donuts. Okay?"

George nodded as the man wrote down his order. The note said, "1 dozen donuts, please."

As George headed to the donut shop, Charkie, a friendly little dog from the neighborhood, joined him. She wanted to play, but George was too busy to stop. So she followed him into the shop.

George noticed that his order only had a little "1" on it. That did not seem like a lot for a monkey who was really hungry. George saw a pencil on the counter. He grabbed it and drew a zero after the "1." Now the note read, "10 dozen donuts."

Then George wrote down another zero before Mrs. D came to take his order.

"George, Charkie, good to see you. Is that an order for your friend with the yellow hat?"

George handed over the paper.

"One hundred dozen donuts!" she exclaimed. "That's our biggest order ever!"

Mrs. D hurried away to tell her husband in the kitchen.

Soon Mrs. D started piling box after box on the counter. George grew worried. He hadn't realized what his zeros would do.

"... Ninety-nine, one hundred. You can't possibly carry them all, George," Mrs. D said. "Lucky for you we have a delivery service!"

14

Mrs. D bustled off to get some help, but George did not wait around. He grabbed one dozen donuts and ran away with Charkie.

George was not quick enough. Mrs. D's entire family was soon right behind him with their towering boxes of donuts.

"He must be running late! We took too long to make the donuts!" Mrs. D cried as she rushed after George.

When George reached his apartment, he jumped from balcony to balcony, trying to get home as quickly as possible.

At first George thought he was safe from the donut delivery. He sat down to catch his breath after running all the way home. But it wasn't long before the doorman showed the D family right up to his apartment!

Soon a hundred boxes of donuts crowded the room. George looked around. He had to do something before his friend came home. Suddenly, he had an idea.

When the man with the yellow hat walked in carrying his groceries, he saw only one box of donuts on the table. "Those smell so good," the man said. "I'm sorry I didn't ask you to buy more than one dozen."

Was George able to hide all those donuts?

Not for long. George explained to the man that he had added some zeros to the order.

"Well, at least you learned something," the man said. "But what are we going to do with all these donuts?"

They came up with a good solution. George got one dozen donuts like he was supposed to . . . and some hard-working firefighters got the rest.

"How many left, George?" the man asked at the end of the day. George ate the last donut from a box and held up his fingers in an "o" shape. Zero!

THE POWER OF TEN

Ask your parent to exchange a one-dollar bill at the bank for two rolls of pennies. Each roll should contain fifty pennies. Using all the coins, make several piles of ten pennies each. How many piles do you end up with? Since you know there are ten pennies in each pile, you can now check to see how many pennies you have by multiplying the number of pile by ten, which means just adding a zero!

See how useful zero can be? It can turn one penny, or one cent, into ten pennies, or ten cents. It can turn ten pennies, or ten cents, into one hundred pennies, or one dollar.

USEFUL FACTS TO REMEMBER:
1 x 10 = 10
10 x 10 = 100
1 penny = 1 cent
10 pennies = 10 cents
100 pennies = 1 dollar

Time to put your pennies into your piggy bank!

TIME TO EAT

Donuts aren't the only thing George likes to eat. George loves to go to Chef Pisghetti's restaurant too! But where is George? Can you find the other items shown?

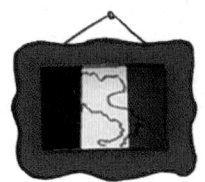

Curious George®
Snowy Day

Adapted by Rotem Moscovich
Based on the TV series teleplay written by Lazar Saric

George woke up to a wonderful surprise. It had snowed all night!

George was curious about all that clean, white snow. Maybe he could build something out of it.

"You go outside, George," said the man with the yellow hat. "I'll make us some cocoa for later."

This was going to be a perfect day. George went out to play. Uh-oh! He sank right into the fluffy powder!

Bill, George's friend and neighbor, came by. He did not have any trouble walking on the snow. "Hey, George," Bill said. "I have an extra pair of cross-country skis you can have."

Then Bill showed George how to ski by making zigzags through the snow. George could not wait to try it for himself.

With skis George could stay on top of the snow, and he followed Bill uphill. Suddenly, they heard a noise. OINK! OINK, OINK, OINK!

Bill said, "I'm going to go find out what that is. You wait here."

George waited on top of the hill in the cold. His house looked so small and warm. George wanted to get home for his cocoa. Was Bill coming back?

"Hey, George!" Bill shouted from the bottom of the hill. "I couldn't find whatever made that sound. But I have to head home now! Keep the skis and have fun!"

So George did . . . for a while.

When George was tired, he skied down the hill toward home—until he hit a rock! His skis flew off, and George tumbled the rest of the way down.

George picked himself up at the bottom of the hill. What would he do now?

He spotted two children pulling a sled. They were walking on the snow—but they did not have skis. How did they do it?

It had to be those wide flat shoes they wore.

"Vinny, I think he likes our snowshoes," the girl said. George nodded.

"Vicky and I live on the other side of the hill," said Vinny. "If you come home with us, we'll lend you our snowshoes so you can get home too. Climb aboard the sled!"

It was fun to sail down another hill, but now George was even farther from his house.

"Here you go, monkey," Vicki said. She gave George her snowshoes and climbed on the sled. "Bye, monkey. Good luck!"

George began his long journey home. He was cold and tired, and climbing up the hill was hard work.

The thought of a nice steaming cup of cocoa kept him going.
   OINK!
   George looked up. There was that noise again. He decided to follow it.

A cold, lost pig!

What was he doing out here all by himself? And how could George rescue the poor pig?

George remembered how Vicki and Vinny had rescued him.

What George needed was a sled. It had to be flat and big enough for the pig to sit on. A fallen sign nearby looked like a good choice.

What a ride!

When George got home, he found his neighbor, Farmer Renkins, talking to the man with the yellow hat.

"Thanks for bringing my pig home, George!" the farmer said. "He got out last night before it snowed."

"Good work, George," said the man with the yellow hat. "There's some cocoa waiting for you inside."

That was exactly what George had hoped to hear.

Skiing, snowshoeing, sledding, and now cocoa . . . it had been the perfect snowy day.

LET IT SNOW!

Make your own snowflake

MATERIALS:
A few sheets of square paper
Safety scissors (or ask an adult for help)

INSTRUCTIONS:

1. Fold the top edge of the paper down to the bottom edge.
2. Fold the left edge over to the right edge.
3. Turn the square so that the corner with all the folds (no open edges!) is at the bottom. Fold the corner on the right side over to the left side, making a triangle.

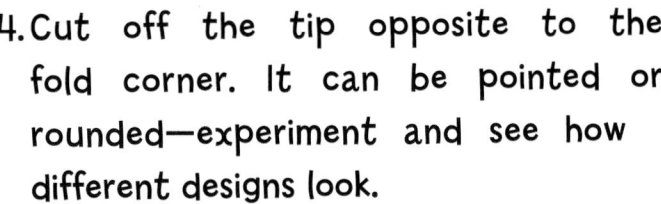

4. Cut off the tip opposite to the fold corner. It can be pointed or rounded—experiment and see how different designs look.
5. Cut out shapes from the edges. The more shapes you cut out, the better.

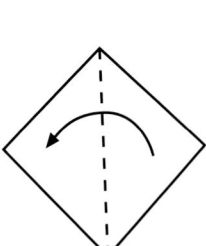

Open up your snowflake when you are finished cutting. You should have a lovely pattern. Now you can paste it on some colored paper, put it up in your window, or hang it on a tree!

Curious George®

The Surprise Gift

Adaptation by Erica Zappy
Based on the TV series teleplay written by Raye Lankford

George was a good little monkey and always very curious. This afternoon George was curious about a large box his friend was bringing home. A large box meant a large gift!

"Sorry, George," said his friend, setting the gift on the table. "This present's not for you. It's for Professor Wiseman's birthday. She'll open it at dinner tonight."

George was disappointed. Dinner was hours away. He wanted to know what was under the wrapping paper right now.

It was lucky George didn't have much time to think about the present. His friend needed help preparing Professor Wiseman's birthday dinner.

"Here is something to unwrap," said his friend. "Peel this orange to get to the good stuff." George took the rind off — SQUIRT! The orange peel had kept the sweet juice inside.

George realized there was a lot of food in the kitchen that could be unwrapped! Bananas, apples, cheese, even an onion — stinky!

Soon George had unwrapped many yummy things. Maybe too many . . .

But he still didn't know what was under the wrapping paper of the gift.

Before George could let his curiosity get the best of him, his friend sent him to the department store to pick up his new suit.

At the store, George encountered many presents. There were gift boxes everywhere he looked, all brightly colored and too tempting for one little monkey to resist.

George unwrapped a box, but there was nothing interesting to him inside.

In the window display, there were more gift boxes. Strangely enough, the boxes had nothing at all inside. They were used for decoration . . . though not anymore!

Now George couldn't wait to help unwrap the present at home. He was sure it would have *something* inside. George hurried to finish his errand.

When George got home, the present was nowhere to be found! The man with the yellow hat had wisely hidden it from his curious little monkey. Did that stop George?

George looked under the table for the surprise gift. Then he went to check the bedrooms and the bathroom.

In the bathroom George noticed that the walls were covered in wrapping paper. George scratched. He peeled. He unwrapped. What did George find after all the unwrapping?

A wall! Unlike presents and fruit, nothing especially good was hiding underneath.

Luckily there was still something left to unwrap that promised something very nice (and very big) inside! It was time for Professor Wiseman to open her birthday gift.

With George's help she unwrapped and unwrapped and unwrapped.

Inside the big box was a small gift. "I never thought a present like this would be in such a big box," she said.

The man with the yellow hat had wrapped it up so that she would have a harder time guessing what was inside. And it worked! George realized that what's on the outside doesn't always tell you what's on the inside!

But sometimes it does.

WHAT'S INSIDE?

George loves unwrapping presents to find out what's inside. But presents aren't the only things that can be unwrapped. Can you point to the wrapping of each item below?

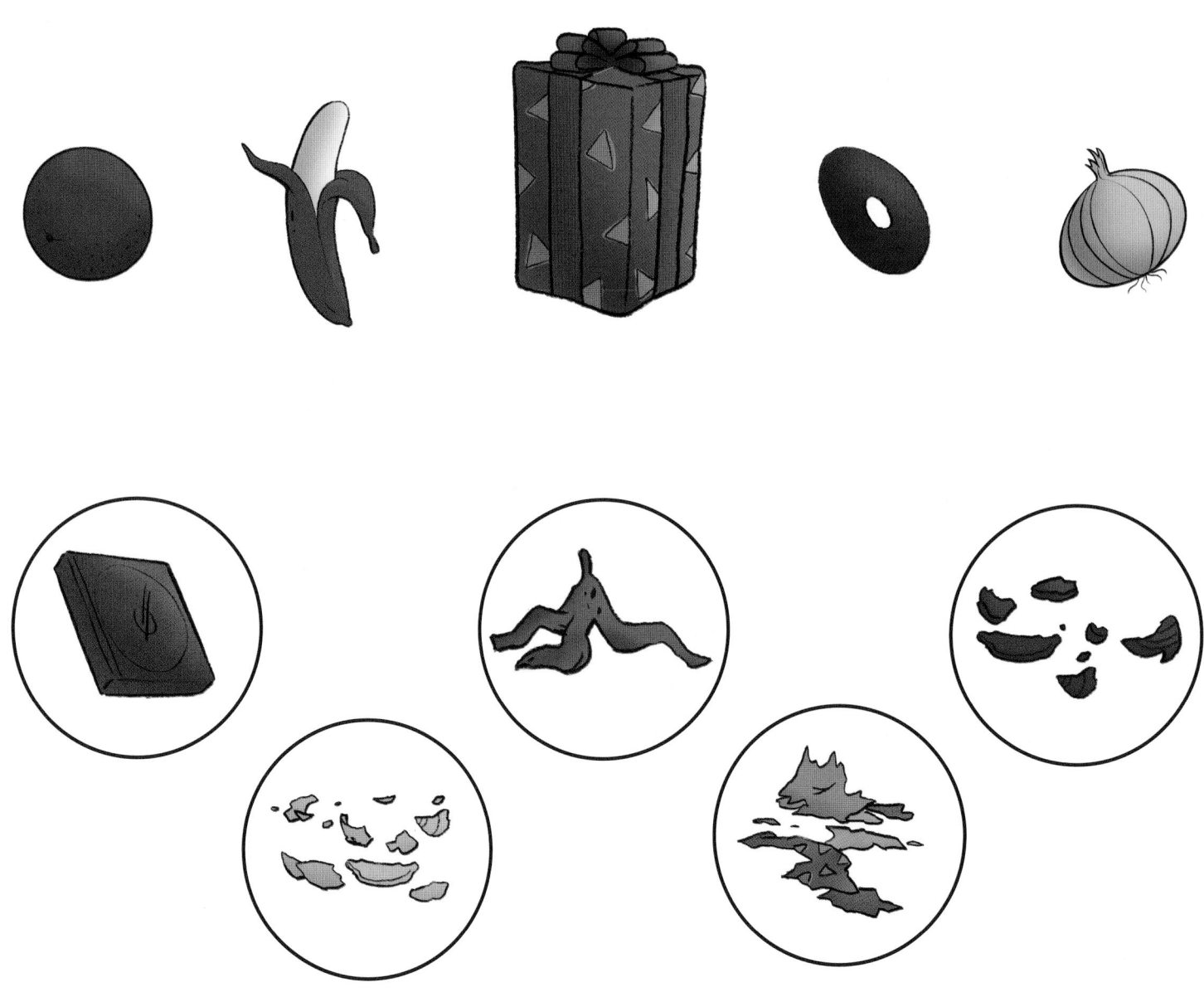

GUESSING GAME

For this activity you will need scissors, tape and newspaper, wrapping paper, or old magazines. Find different-size boxes and containers in your house and put something inside. Then wrap them up! When you are finished wrapping, see if a parent or friend can guess what is inside. They can shake it, feel how heavy it is, and even ask twenty questions: Is it something I can eat? Is it bigger than a cookie? See how clues such as size and weight help you determine what you might find on the inside!

THINK MORE ABOUT IT

Can you find things in your house that are already "wrapped"? Do your favorite cookies come inside a bag? Maybe that bag is inside a box. What about your favorite cereal? And where do you keep your toys? Are they inside something else? Why do you think some things are wrapped?

Curious George®

The Boat Show

Adaptation by Kate O'Sullivan
Based on the TV series teleplay
written by Raye Lankford

It was a beautiful day and
George was curious.
He was curious about all the
boats on the river.

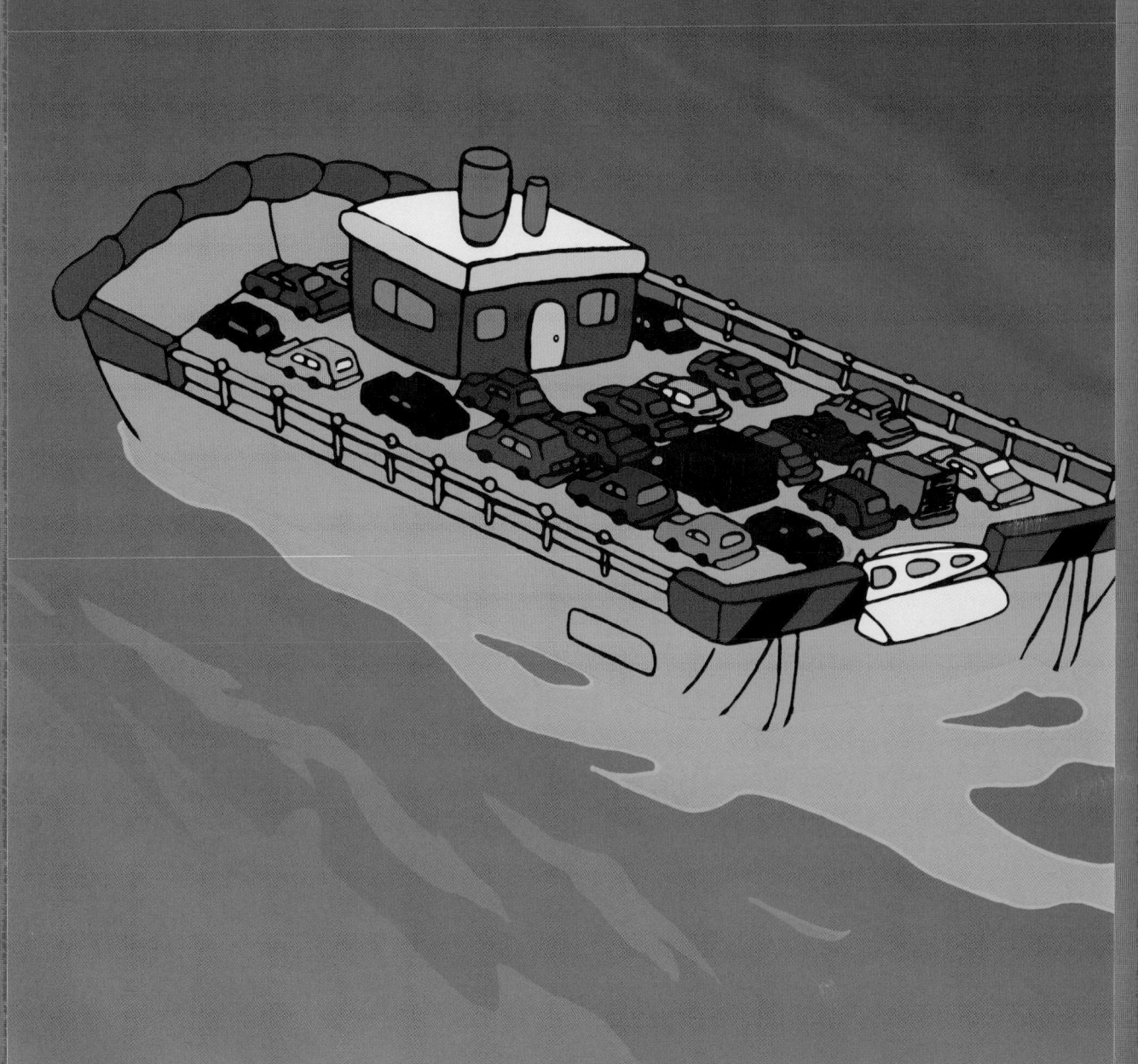

George liked one boat best of all.
It was carrying cars!
"That is a ferryboat," said the
man with the yellow hat.

George liked to boat watch but
he was eager to get to the lake.
If he was lucky, he might see
another ferryboat.

At the lake
there were lots of people.
They were watching the model
boat contest.
There were boats of all kinds.

Bill showed George his model sailboat.
George thought it was wonderful.

"I saved a lot of money to build this boat," Bill said.
"Will you keep it safe until the contest?"

George was happy to help.
He held the boat very carefully.

He looked at the boat.
He looked at his toy cars.
George had an idea.

George made Bill's boat look just like a ferryboat.

Oh, no! It sank.
What would Bill enter into the contest now?

George tried to make another
boat for Bill out of his toys.
It sank, too.
George saw that some of the
toys floated.
He had a better idea.

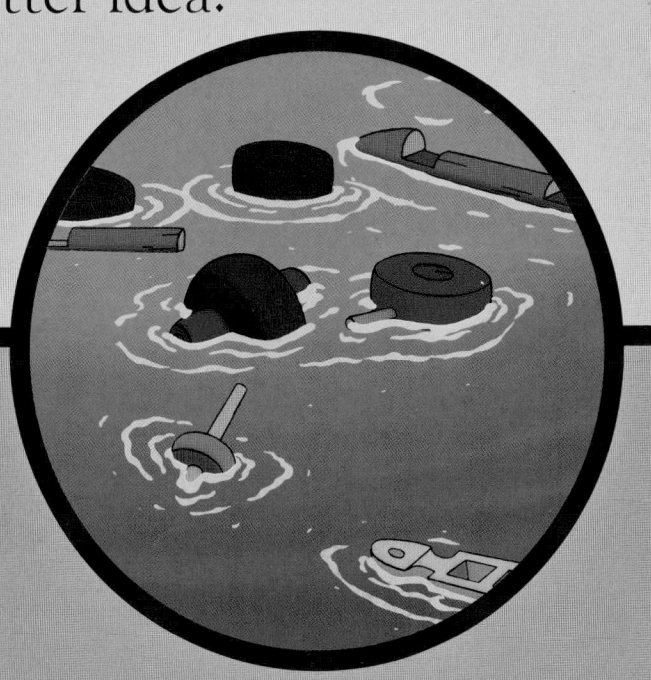

George looked at other boats
on the river.
He made plans to build a boat
from his floating toys.
Bill would be proud.

When Bill came back, he saw the
new boat.
"That is a great ferryboat!" Bill said.

Then George showed Bill what
had happened to the sailboat.

"Uh-oh!" Bill said.
"I forgot to shut the boat's windows.
I'll fix that.

Now water cannot get inside and the boat will float.
Let's go enter our boats in the contest!"

Everyone won a blue ribbon
for all their hard work—even
George.

SHIPS AHOY!

Make a paper boat.

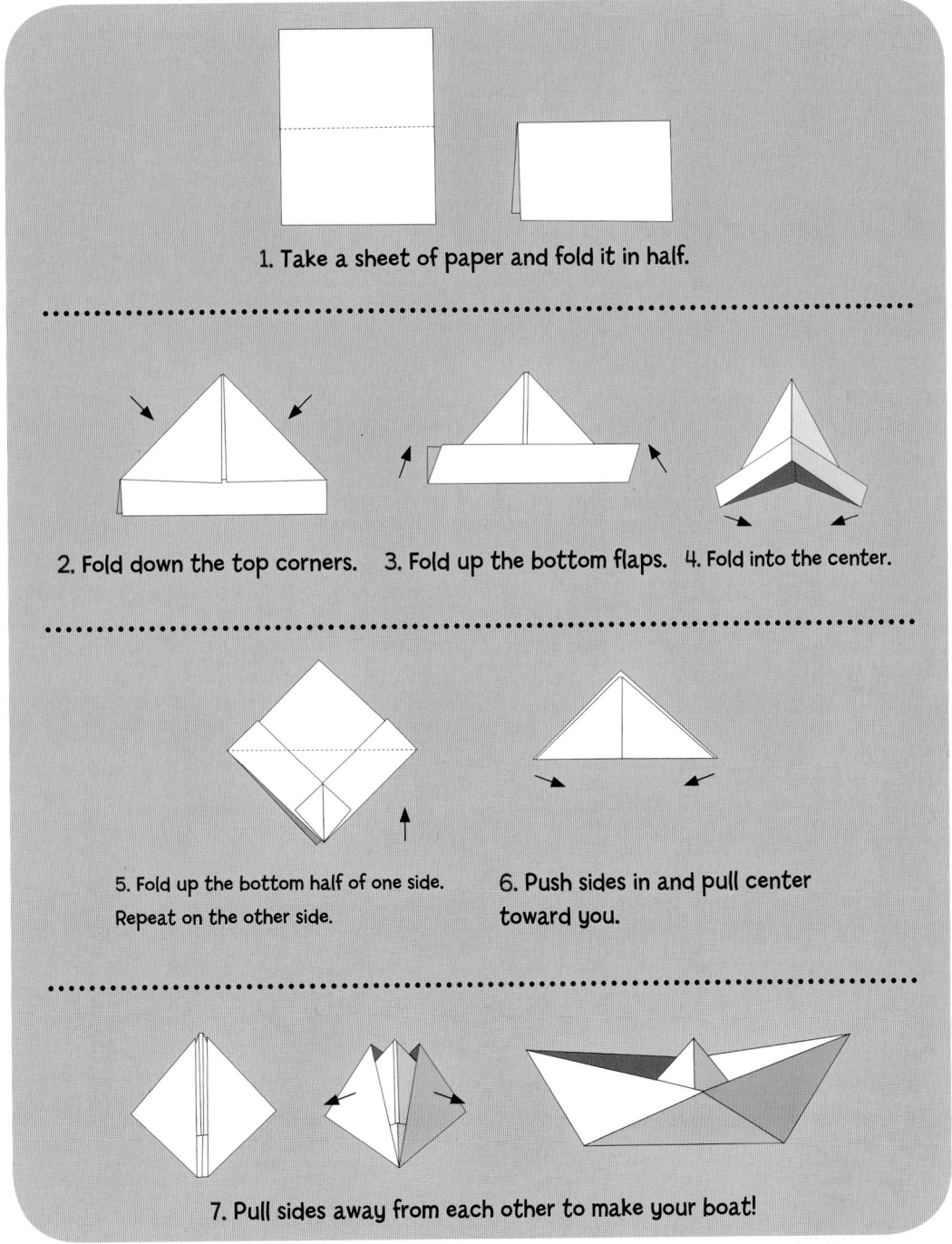

1. Take a sheet of paper and fold it in half.

2. Fold down the top corners.   3. Fold up the bottom flaps.   4. Fold into the center.

5. Fold up the bottom half of one side.
Repeat on the other side.

6. Push sides in and pull center toward you.

7. Pull sides away from each other to make your boat!

Now test your boat and see if it floats.

SAIL AWAY

Curious George is helping Bill sail his model sailboat. Can you help George spot these other fun items?

Curious George®

Builds a Home

Adaptation by Monica Perez
Based on the TV series teleplay written by Joe Fallon

It was a perfect day for sitting on the balcony, eating grapes, drinking juice, and drawing—all at the same time. George was a good little monkey who was good at many things. He was especially good at being curious.

Today George was curious about a bird. He had seen a lot of pigeons, but none wearing an ankle tag.

The pigeon had seen a lot of animals, but none drawing on a sketchpad. They spent the morning watching each other.

"George, this is your best drawing yet!" George's best friend, the man with the yellow hat, told him. "That tag the bird is wearing means that it is a homing pigeon. They're special birds that always return home."

George looked hopeful.

"Homing pigeons have special homes," the man added. "Our apartment is not a good home for a bird."

George saw that what his pigeon needed most was a place to roost.
A tree would be perfect. George came up with a great way to get a tree up to
his apartment. He would build one.

Uh-oh! The tree George built of pipe cleaners was not strong enough for a pigeon to sit on.

George thought of another idea. With clay, George could make a tree as big and thick as he wanted.

But George must have used too much water because the tree made of clay did not hold its shape.

George decided he needed more information to build the perfect tree, so he went to the park. He looked at the trees for a long time. He drew trees on a piece of paper.

Then he began a new project.

It took him a long time to build, but finally George revealed his masterpiece. It looked almost like a real tree. Baseball bats were the roots, and a coat rack was the trunk. A frayed brown rope was its bark.

Toilet paper and rubber gloves hung off it like leaves. George had even added real soil. George's friend the pigeon hopped onto a branch. He settled in.

That afternoon the man with the yellow hat brought home a guest. It was the doorman. He had lost one of his pigeons that he kept on the roof.

When they entered the apartment, they found . . . a big mess!

"George!" the man with the yellow hat exclaimed. "Is that—a tree?"
George nodded proudly. Now that he had the perfect home, the bird could live
with them forever.

But the doorman had missed his pigeon. When he called out, "Compass!" the happy bird flew right into his hands.

Poor George! He waved goodbye to Compass and the doorman. Then he sat alone on the balcony. The man with the yellow hat placed a potted tree on the ground. "I bought it for the birds to sit in so you can draw them," he said, trying to cheer George up.

George shook his head and pointed to his own tree.
The man said, "It was a good effort, George, but birds want to sit in a real tree."

But to George's delight, the birds did not agree with his friend. Not at all!

BUILD A HOME

George followed a series of logical steps in order to build his pigeon roost.
Engineers use a similar process for technology design:
1. Start with a problem—state what needs to be designed or built.
2. Develop a design, or make a sketch, for solving the problem.
3. Build a model. If it works, great! If it doesn't, make changes to your design and try again. Be patient—it may take several tries.

Can you point to the first step, and the second, and so on?

ANSWER: 1.  2.  3.  4.  5.  6.

Curious George®
Lost and Found

Adaptation by Erica Zappy
Based on the TV series teleplay written by Joe Fallon

It was the weekend, and George was excited. He and his friend had left the city for their country house.

After a long drive, George was happy to arrive. He was looking forward to feeding the ducks.

"Don't wander far, George," said the man with the yellow hat as their neighbor Mrs. Renkins drove up to say hello.

But someone else had wandered off—Mrs. Renkins's chicks! George's friend offered to help find them. Meanwhile, George headed toward the river.

At the river, George fed the ducks with his friend Jumpy Squirrel. They found a raft that let them get closer to their duck friends . . .

. . . so close that George felt just like a duck as he floated down the river.
Uh-oh! The raft had drifted away from the shore!

George enjoyed his trip down the river with all of his hungry duck friends.

But Jumpy was worried. They were lost, just like the chicks.

The raft passed some crooked trees and a big rock that looked like a duck.

The big duck rock made the ducks quack and George smile, but Jumpy was too worried to sightsee. The sun was setting. How were they going to find their way back to the farm?

When they reached a bend in the river, George and Jumpy spotted a silo.

Hooray! It looked like the Renkinses' farm!

They waited until the raft neared the shore, then jumped off and headed toward the silo. But it wasn't the right farm. The Renkinses' silo was red.

They were still lost. They looked around. Nothing looked familiar. Except . . . THE BIG DUCK ROCK!

It was a landmark. Maybe it would help them find their way home.

George drew a map.

He remembered the big duck rock, the crooked trees, and the silo at the Renkinses' farm. George also remembered that the sun set behind the red silo every night.

George and Jumpy decided they should follow the sun. It would help them find their way back to the farm, especially if they looked for other landmarks along the way.

As George and Jumpy walked back to the farm, Jumpy bumped into their friends who were lost . . . the chicks!

The chicks did not understand how to use landmarks to navigate, but they were happy to follow the squirrel and monkey back to the farm.

At the farm, Mrs. Renkins and the man with the yellow hat were surprised when George and Jumpy showed up with the chicks in tow.

"George, weren't you supposed to be feeding the ducks?" asked the man with the yellow hat. George tried to explain.

But it was easier to let the chicks do all the squawking!

FIND YOUR WAY

When George got lost, he made a map so he could find his way home. Maps are usually drawn on a flat surface, such as a sheet of paper, and use pictures or symbols to show you where real places are located. You can make a map, too, of your bedroom, your backyard, or even your neighborhood.

To Make a Treasure Map

You will need these things:

- Sheets of paper (white is best)
- Markers or crayons
- A treasure!

1. Pick a secret spot in your backyard and hide something — that's the treasure.

2. Draw the outline of your backyard and then draw the important things that are in it. Here are some examples of landmarks: a swing set, trees, a swimming pool, a garden, a patio, or a shed.

3. Mark the spot where you've hidden the treasure with an "X" on your map, and give the maps to your friends or family. See who can find the treasure first!

Curious George®

Plays Mini Golf

Adaptation by Marcy Goldberg Sacks
Based on the TV series teleplay
written by Craig Miller

George and Steve were good friends.
They liked to play games.
Steve always had the high score.
He always won.

One day Steve invited George to play mini golf.
This was a new game for George.
He was curious.
Maybe he could win this time.

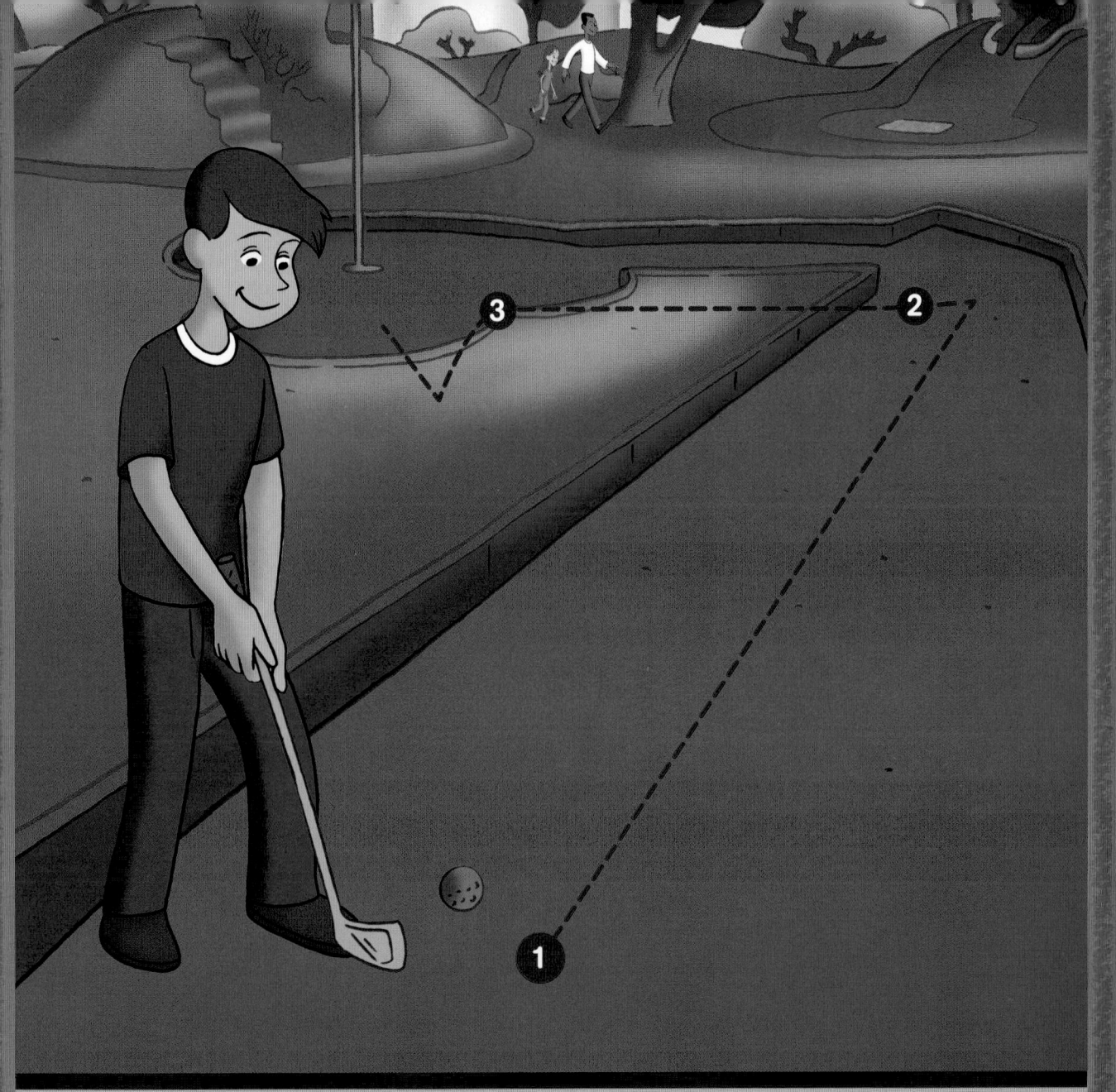

Steve hit the ball one . . . two . . .
three times.
Now it was George's turn.

George took a big swing.
His ball hit two trees!

George swung his golf club
many times to get a high score.

George hit the ball again and
again and again.

It went all over the golf course.
Golf was easy!

George hit the ball as many times
as he could.
Finally, he hit it right into the hole.

At the end of the game, Steve read
the scores: Steve, 35, Betsy, 58,
and George . . . 250!

George had the highest score.
He was so happy.
He had won.

"But George, in golf the *lowest* score is best," Betsy told him. "I won the game," Steve said.

George was surprised.
How could a small number be
better than a big number?

George had an idea.
He wanted to win in golf.
He had to practice.
George asked his friend if he
could borrow some things from
their house.

George made a golf course on the roof!
A paper towel roll was his club.
He blew in one end.
Air came out the other end.

The ball moved.
He was ready to play.
George invited Steve over.

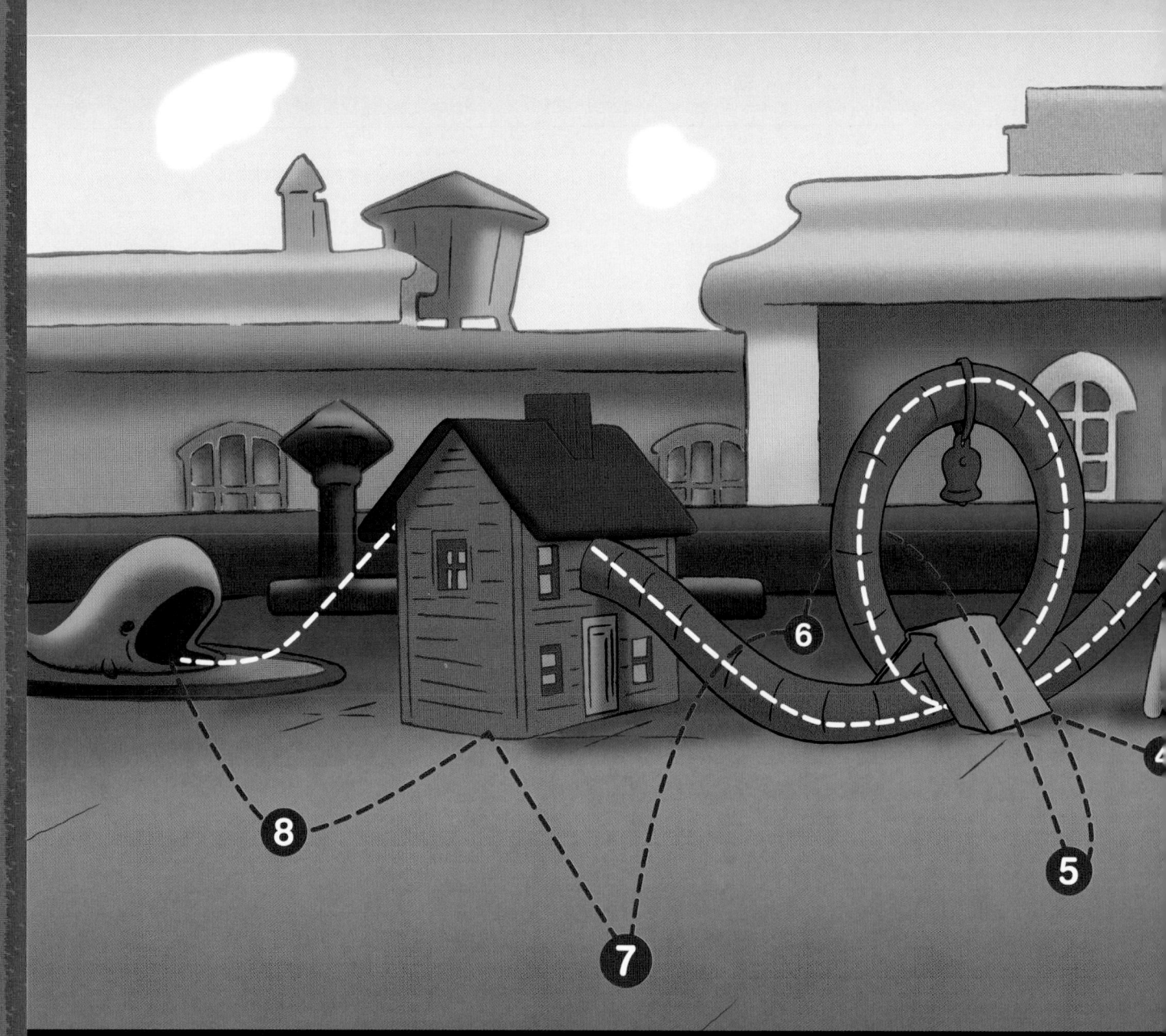

George played first.
He blew through the tube . . . and
got a hole in one!

Steve was next.
But it took him eight tries to get
the ball into the hole.

Steve counted the points.
George had the lowest score.
Finally he was the winner—of
monkey mini golf!

MINI MINI GOLF

George used "found objects" to make his own mini golf course. You can do the same using household items like these:

ruler and dry sponge, rubber ball or marbles, paper, tape, scissors, cardboard boxes, paper towel rolls, cotton towels, paper plates, a coffee can, building blocks, or other toys

INSTRUCTIONS:

1. Make a golf club by taping a dry sponge to the bottom of a ruler.

2. Draw pictures of your ideas for a golf course. Choose one you can build with materials you have.

3. Build your course (see ideas below), using the coffee can as the final hole.

4. Take turns with a friend playing your way through.

5. Talk about what's working and what's not. Do you need to change your design?

IDEAS FOR YOUR GOLF COURSE:

- Make a tunnel by taping a paper towel roll on the floor.
- Put a chair or stool in the room for your ball to go under.
- Place paper plates on the floor to create obstacles for your ball to go around.
- Make a "sand trap" from a towel.
- Use two rows of building blocks to create a straight pathway.
- Come up with your own creative ideas!

Curious George®
Tadpole Trouble

Adaptation by Mark London Williams
Based on the TV series teleplay written by Bruce Akiyama

George was exploring a lake with his friend Bill. George was a good explorer, and always very curious.

He was especially curious about tadpoles.

Bill told George he could be in charge of the tadpoles they found.

George took tadpole-watching very seriously. He watched them swim in their glass bowl. He fed them boiled lettuce.

He took them for a swim in the lake. At the time it seemed like good exercise for tadpoles.

When the tadpoles did not come back, George started to worry. What would Bill say? He had to find them.

George spent hours at the lake. He found turtles, and water beetles, and minnows. But no tadpoles.

Every time George would visit the lake he would look for the tadpoles. Several weeks went by.

Finally he found something that looked like a tadpole — but it had legs, and almost no tail. George let it go.

A few weeks after that, George took a walk in the city to think about his tadpole problem. He was going back to the lake soon. Bill would be very disappointed if George had lost the tadpoles.

George walked so long, he found himself in front of the museum. He saw a butterfly that reminded him of being at the lake. He followed it.

The butterfly flew into the museum and George kept following, past all kinds of exhibits.

There was a special display about creatures that live around lakes. George knew about many of them, like turtles, minnows, lizards . . . and tadpoles!

The picture of the baby tadpole reminded him of his own tadpoles. Next to it was one of the funny creatures George had seen in the lake. It had legs and a smaller tail.

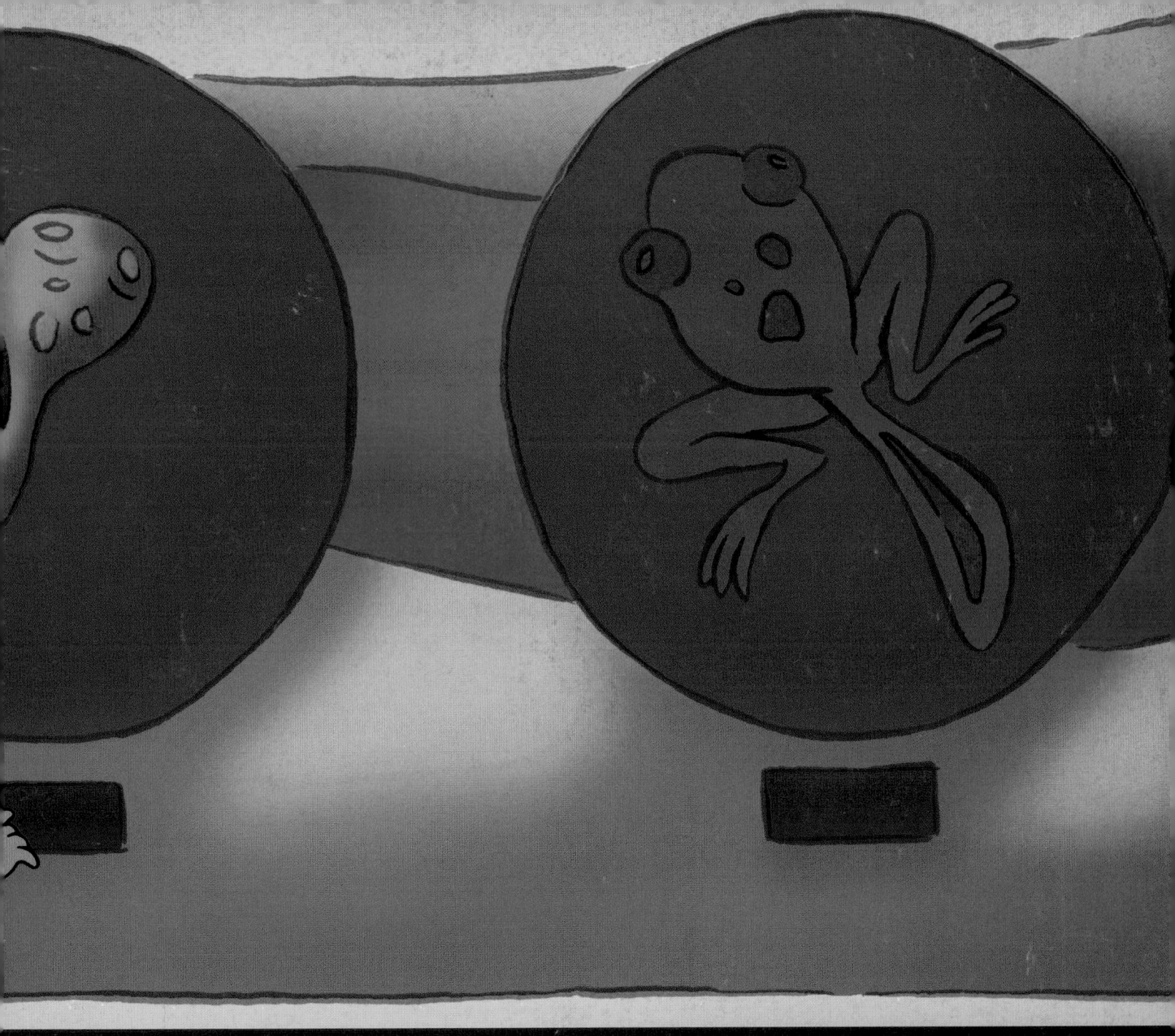

Now he understood! The creatures with legs were tadpoles, too! His friends had not vanished. They were just changing and growing up. George was so excited, he left the museum without finishing the exhibit tour.

As soon as George got back to the lake, he looked for his missing friends. Especially the ones with little legs and almost no tails.

But they were not there, either. This time George could find only . . . frogs! Lots and lots of frogs!

"What a good idea, George," Bill said, seeing the empty jar.

"You decided to release the tadpoles into their natural habitat so we could watch them grow into frogs. You're not only curious—you're smart, too!"

"Let's take a picture of you and the frogs together, George. Smile!"

THE LIFE OF A BUTTERFLY

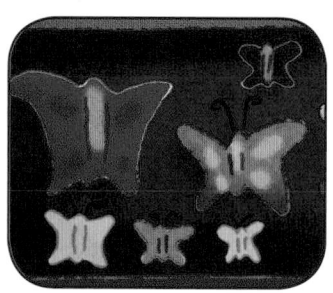

The life cycle of a butterfly is as amazing as the frog's. The butterfly begins life as an egg, which hatches into a caterpillar. A caterpillar eats leaves and sheds its old skin several times as it grows. When it is large enough, it hangs from a leaf and forms a hard outer shell called a chrysalis. A butterfly emerges from the chrysalis!

Here are simple instructions to make your own caterpillar. You will need:

CARDBOARD EGG CARTON
LONG COLORED PIPE CLEANERS
MARKERS OR CRAYONS

1. Take the empty egg carton and cut off the top of the box.
2. Turn the bottom of the carton upside down. With a sharp pencil, poke several holes along the sides of the carton. Make the same number of holes on each side.
3. Insert pipe cleaners in one hole on one side of the carton and out the hole on the opposite side of the carton.
4. Bend the pipe cleaners in an L shape on each side. These are the caterpillar's legs!
5. Now you can draw eyespots on the front of your caterpillar and even poke two extra holes to insert pipe cleaners for its antennae.
6. Many caterpillars are brightly colored with stripes, so have fun decorating your new friend with marker or crayons!

BUTTERFLY FRIENDS

George loves butterflies! Use your finger to trace the lines below to find out which path will lead George to his butterfly friends.

US LUCKY BRIGHT CURI
GE BRIGHT SWEET GEO
MISCHIEVOUS CURIOUS
AVE LUCKY NICE BRAV
VOUS CURIOUS MISCH
US LUCKY BRIGHT CURI
GE BRIGHT SWEET GEO
MISCHIEVOUS CURIOUS
LUCKY GEORGE BRAVE
VOUS CURIOUS MISCH
US LUCKY BRIGHT CURI

MUSEUM MONKEY

George is at the museum store looking for a picture of one of his favorite animals. Can you help him find the dinosaur and the other items shown?

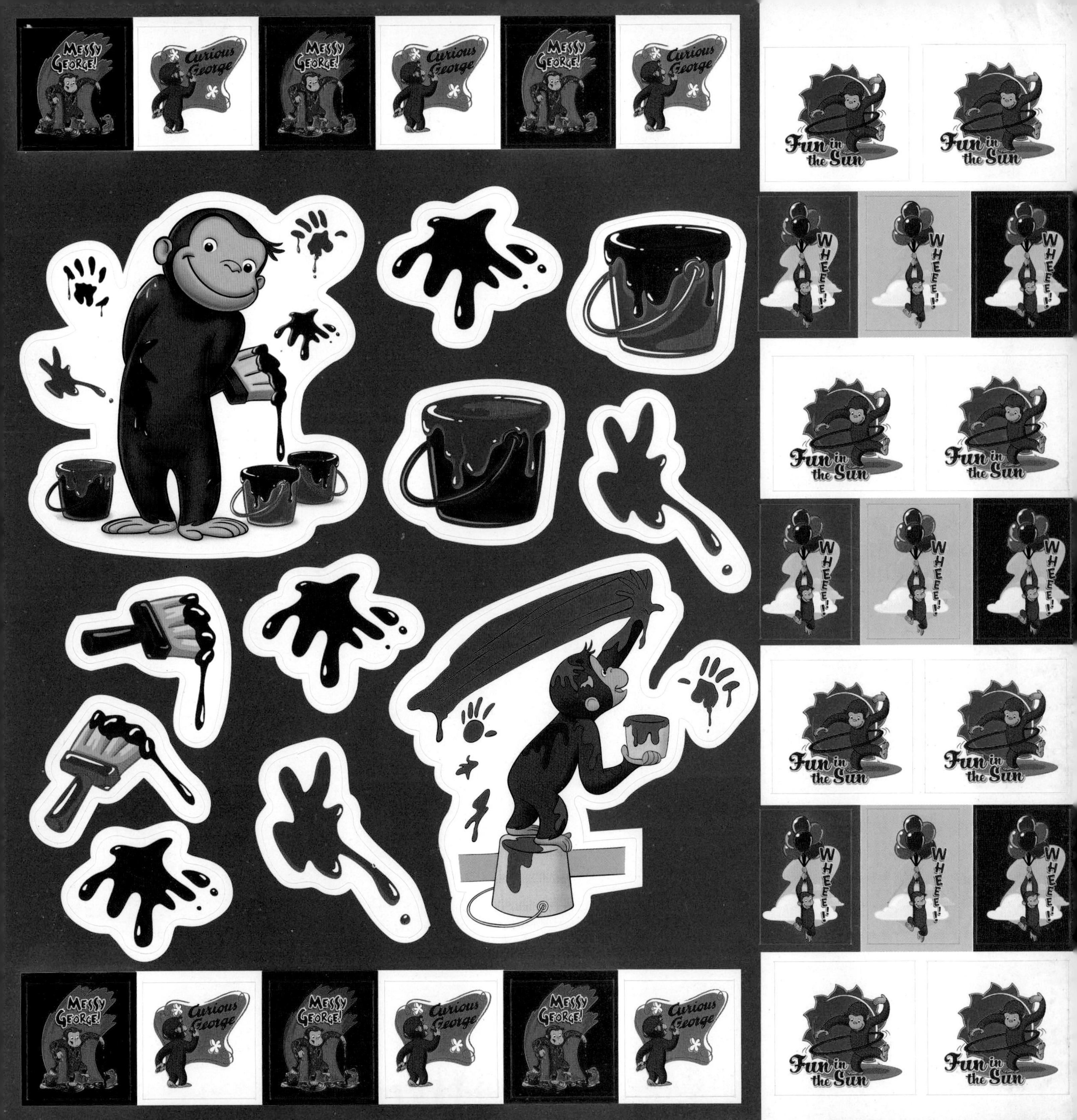
MESSY GEORGE!
Curious George
Fun in the Sun
WHEEE!

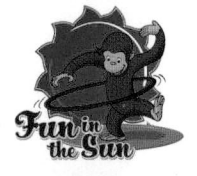

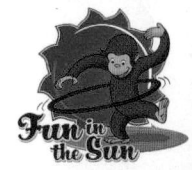

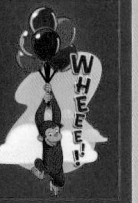

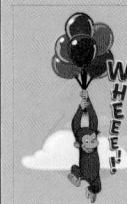

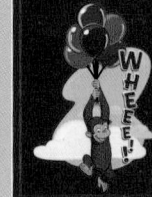

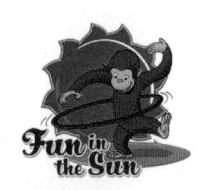

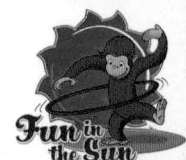

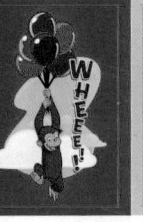

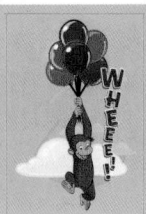

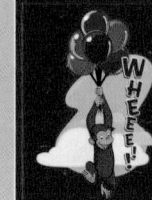

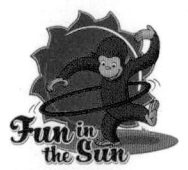

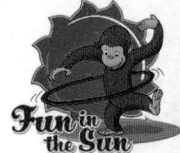

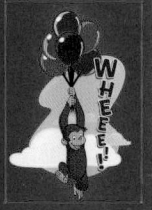

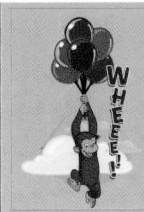

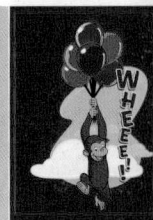

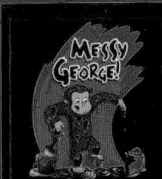

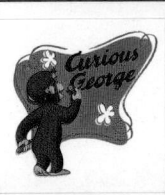

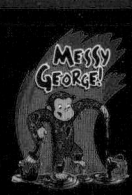

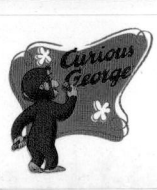

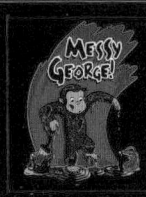

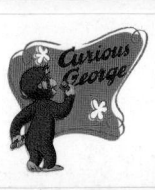

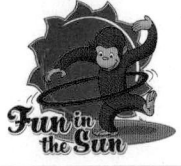

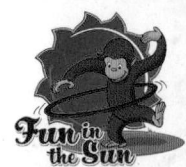